# Ask a Silly Question
# and Other Poems

I knocked a vase of flowers
over Dad's chair
the other day;
he was sitting there
at the time.

'Just look at me,' he shouted
'I'm wet!
I'll skin you alive, my lad
Get upstairs to bed,
no arguing!'

IRENE RAWNSLEY

# Ask a Silly Question

*Illustrated by Simone Abel*

*For Ann
Best wishes,
Irene Rawnsley
8.3.93*

**MAMMOTH**

For Katy

First published in 1988
by Methuen Children's Books Ltd.
First published in 1989 by Mammoth
an imprint of Mandarin Paperbacks
Michelin House, 81 Fulham Road, London SW3 6RB
Text copyright © 1988 Irene Rawnsley
Illustrations copyright © 1988 Simone Abel
Printed in Great Britain by
Cox & Wyman Ltd, Reading

ISBN 0 7497 0005 X

A CIP catalogue record for this title is available
from the British Library

This paperback is sold subject to the condition
that it shall not, by way of trade or otherwise,
be lent, re-sold, hired out or otherwise
circulated without the publisher's prior
consent in any form of binding or cover
other than that in which it is published and
without a similar condition including this condition
being imposed on the subsequent purchaser.

# Contents

**Me and My Family**
Staying Up  7
At the Party  9
Page One  11
Painting  13
Treasure Trove  14
Intruder  16
My Brother and the Ragman  18
Mum and Dad and Me  21
Interesting Things  23
Time to Dust the Daffodils  24
Changing his Mind  27

**In School**
Why I'm Late  28
Brayns  30
Ask a Silly Question  31
Changing Places  32
Plants in the Classroom  34
The Visitor  37
Teacher's Pet  38
Copycat  40
A Caterpillar  42
Where Miss Apple Goes  45

**In the Playground**
A Nut up my Nose   46
Trouble   49
Sailing my Boat   50
Nobody to Play With   52
Flying   53

**Out and About**
Weather   55
Butterfly Calypso   57
Easy Mover   58
Storm   59
Ginger   60
Brave   63
Countdown   64

# Me and My Family

## Staying Up

One night
when I complained
it was too early for bed
Mum said, 'All right then.
Stay up late.'

It was good at first.
I watched
the jokey T.V. people
sing and laugh
and do their stuff,

then Mum began to yawn:
'Me, I'm tired.
I'm going to bed.
Please turn off the set
when you come up.'

The room felt strange
with only me
and the talking T.V. people
watching
from their box.

Even when I switched off
they were still there;
hurrying to bed
I felt their breath
behind me on the stair.

# At the Party

Leave me alone!
I don't want to dance.
I would have stayed away
from this party
if they'd given me a chance.

The sight of jelly
makes me sick.
Why did Peter pick on me
to come to his birthday?
He doesn't even like me.

These silver shoes
are giving me blisters.
I hate my dress,
it was once my sister's
and she's much fatter than I am.

I spent all my money
on a Super Space Game;
two other guests
brought exactly the same
and Peter says he's already got one.

I'm not going to join
in their stupid fun;
until Dad comes to take me home
I'm just going to sit here,
ON MY OWN!

# Page One

Jim and Jane go to the seaside.
It is sunny. They do not fight.
They play with Rags the dog.
He does not bite.

Mummy and Daddy smile.
The toy shop lady smiles.
The man in the café smiles.
Jim and Jane smile.
Rags smiles.
They all smile, in reading books.

# Painting

Yellow is my favourite colour;
I'm painting like the sun,
Yellow birds in golden bushes
Till all the yellow's done.

Green is my favourite colour;
I'm painting like the grass,
Green woods and fields and rushes,
The river flowing past.

Blue is my favourite colour;
I'm painting like the sea,
Blue sailing ships and fishes,
And icebergs floating free.

Red is my favourite colour;
I'm painting like a fire,
Red twigs, then blazing branches
As the flames leap higher.

# Treasure Trove

I have a tin
to keep things in
underneath
my bedroom floor.

I put my finger
in the crack,
quietly lift
the floorboard back,

and there's my store,
safely hid
in a tin with roses
on the lid.

A few feathers
and a chicken's claw,
a big tooth
from a dinosaur,

the wrapper
from my Easter egg,
a Christmas robin
with one leg,

long hairs
from a horse's mane,
real pesetas
come from Spain,

three of my
operation stitches,
like spiders
wrapped in bandages,

a marble
full of dragon smoke,
flashing with fire
in the dark,

a magic pebble
round and white,
a sparkler left
from bonfire night.

Underneath
my bedroom floor
there's a treasure tin,
with my things in.

# Intruder

Just now I heard
a man whistling;
he stopped when he knew
I was listening.

The cat on the bed
turned his head
to the door,
stiffened his hair;
what did he do that for
if nobody's there?

# My Brother
# And the Ragman

There's a ragman
comes down our street
with silver windmills
and balloons on sticks;
all the kids want one.

All you have to do
is take a bundle
of tatty old clothes,
throw them on the cart,
then he lets you choose.

One day he'd run out
of windmills and balloons
so he brought goldfish
in little plastic bags
full of water.

The trouble was,
we couldn't get any rags.
Mum was at the shops;
she'd locked up
and left us in the garden.

'Don't worry!' said my brother,
and right there
he took off his socks,
his jumper and vest
and ran to the cart.

We got our fish.
When Mum came home
we were sitting on the step
holding the bag,
deciding on his name.

You should have seen Mum's face!
Straightaway she sent
my brother to bed
and me to buy a bowl
and a packet of food.

We've still got Flash.
Every night we tap on the glass
saying his name
and he swims to us
for his dinner.

What we haven't got
is any pocket money.
Mum is making us pay
for new clothes
and it will take until Christmas.

She says we could have had
a fish for Christmas,
if only we'd asked.
Maybe she'll buy us one in any case.
Flash would like a friend.

# Mum and Dad and Me

I knocked a vase of flowers
over Dad's chair
the other day;
he was sitting there
at the time.

'Just look at me,' he shouted,
'I'm wet!
I'll skin you alive, my lad
Get upstairs to bed,
no arguing!'

But Mum calmed him down,
mopped him up,
made a fresh brew,
said, 'If your son's clumsy
he takes after you.'

Today I painted those flowers,
purple and red;
the teacher said
I could bring my picture home.
Mum was pleased.

'If I were you I would
pin it up for Dad to see.
You're very good
at painting, my lad,
you take after me!'

# Interesting Things

Our dog
can walk on two legs.
My brother
can stand on his head.
My sister
can skate on one foot.
Grandma
can knit with one hand.
My dad
can lift me with one finger.
And me,
I can read this poem
with both eyes closed!

# Time to Dust the Daffodils

My gran's too old
to go out
in the cold garden
planting bulbs,
but she likes
spring flowers.

She has a box
of plastic daffodils
on sticks
that she hides away
in the winter.

When she notices
that spring is coming
she takes them out,
dusts each one
carefully,

then plants them
underneath her window.

Passers-by pause
to admire them.
'How lovely, Mrs Paradine!
Why do your daffodils
always bloom earlier
than mine?'

# Changing his Mind

'Yes means no
and no means yes,'
said my brother
on the way to the park,
making conversation.

Mum gave us bread
for the ducks
but he said no,
he wouldn't feed them,
and no to sailing boats,

and no to skimming stones
across the water,
no to the roundabout
the swings and slide,

but he cried
when he didn't get an ice cream.
'Yes means yes
and no means no,'
said my brother.

# In School

## Why I'm Late

Please, Miss Apple,
don't be cross;
I'm late because
I missed the bus;
this time it wasn't my fault, truly.

Last night Dad brought
a puppy home;
we call him Sam.
He's a little beauty
but he's into all kinds of mischief.

He pulled the threads
from the rug in the hall,
scratched the patterns
from the kitchen wall,
savaged the curtains,
chewed Dad's slippers,
ate the kippers we were
going to have for tea,
then fell asleep in the coal bucket.

'That dog needs exercise,'
said my dad,
but he didn't have a collar
or a lead,
so I went to buy them this morning,
with my pocket money.

That's why I walked
to school today;
my legs are aching,
it's a very long way.
That's how I came
to miss the bus.

Please, Miss Apple,
don't be cross.

# Brayns

Im mils mor clevver
than enniwun els
Thers milions of brayns
in mi hed,
I can mayk modls
that reelly wurk
And big kyts
to fli over hed.

My picturs ar beter
than orl the rest,
But I ownli got two
in the speling test.

# Ask a Silly Question

'Children,
What are you running for?'
Asked the cross teacher
In the corridor.

'Please Miss,'
Said cheeky Jenny Patchett,
'My pen's run out –
We're trying to catch it!'

# Changing Places

Please, Miss Apple,
May I sit next to Jane?
I don't like Richard any more.
He borrows my things without asking,
And loses them on the floor.

Please, Miss Apple,
May I sit next to Eric?
I didn't like Jane for very long.
She copied my column of answers
Then complained when they were all wrong.

Please, Miss Apple,
May I sit next to Lee?
Eric won't stay in his place.
He spreads out his work into my half,
And he doesn't leave me any space.

Please, Miss Apple,
May I sit next to Gary?
It isn't much fun next to Lee.
He's always singing and whistling;
I'm afraid you might think it's me.

Please, Miss Apple,
May I sit next to Veronica?
Gary's been picking a fight.
He says that I took the best paintbrush.
He's going to get me tonight.

Please, Miss Apple,
May I sit next to Tracey?
Veronica's making me sick.
She keeps chewing a bit off her lolly,
And refuses to give me a lick.

Please, Miss Apple,
May I sit next to Richard?
I'm sure we won't argue again;
I've got some new sports cards to show him;
Besides, Tracey's sitting with Ben.

# Plants in the Classroom

Plants in the classroom seem to say,
'We've not been watered today.'

What must they think,
Standing above the sink,
When they hear how the water gushes,
And you're only washing the brushes?

It's a daily habit,
Giving fresh water
To the rabbit.

Even the fish
Have their wish,
Every Friday when the tank is scrubbed.
Plants must think that they've been snubbed;

Not a drop of water
Comes their way.
They see you carefully watering the clay

But to them
Not a dribble.
They'd climb out of their pots
If they were able,

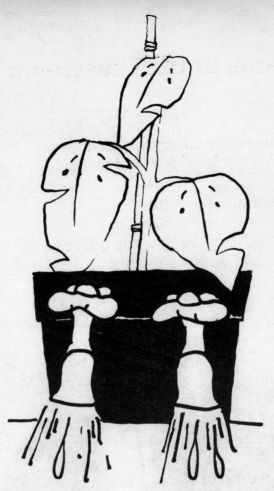

Step down from their ledges,
Balance on the edges of the water trough,
Drink and drink till they'd had enough.

But they can't.
So they stay where they've been put,
Quietly withering away.

# The Visitor

In the Wendy House today
a great big, sleepy, fat cat
was curled on the cushion.
Nobody knew his name
or where he had come from.

When we gently woke him
he stretched his long front legs,
curved his claws and yawned;
such fierce teeth, but he was friendly,
rubbing against us, purring.

All morning we kept him.
He drank milk from little saucers,
jumped on the table, upset the cups,
played games with the pastry,
chased the rolling pin.

Then, quick as light,
he was gone through the window.
Miss Apple said, 'He'll be back soon,
for more milk.' But he hasn't come.
Nobody knows where he has gone.

# Teacher's Pet

Why does Tracey Johnson
Wear neat, new clothes,
And a tartan dress
With matching bows?

Why does she bring chocolates
And sweets galore
To offer to the teachers
At the staffroom door?

Why is it always Tracey
Who gives out the number cards,
Answers all the questions,
Gets the most gold stars?

When it's freezing in the yard
And we're sent outdoors,
Why can she sort the bookshelf
And tidy out the drawers?

Tracey Johnson, Tracey Johnson
With her stuck-up smile;
I wish I could be Tracey Johnson
For a while.

# Copycat

Every time we have painting
Jonathan copies me.

Today I did a red house
with a chimney on top,
made smoke come out,
put curtains at the window,
a cat on the doorstep,
a tree in the garden
with one blackbird,
a path, a gate,
and a big sun shining.

When I looked at his picture
Jonathan had copied me.

He had a red house,
a smoking chimney,
a cat on the doorstep,
curtains at the window,
a garden, a tree
with a blackbird perched
on the same branch,
a path leading to a gate
and a big sun shining.

The teacher said, 'Which of you copied?'
But I didn't tell.
Jonathan's a copycat
but he's my friend as well.

# A Caterpillar

I found a caterpillar once;
I put him in a jar to show my mum.
She said he must always have
raspberry leaves to eat
or he would die.

I took him to school
to put on the Nature Table;
every morning I took
fresh raspberry leaves
for him to eat.

One morning he was gone.
There were the stalks
of yesterday's leaves
but he was nowhere.
'He's under the lid,' said Miss.

And so he was,
tucked neatly away
in a silky white sleeping bag,
caterpillar-size,
that he'd made for himself.

I forgot him for a while,
stopped taking
fresh leaves to school
and looking in the jar,
but it stayed in its place.

It was a big surprise
when he turned into a moth.
During sums I was sitting
at the front, near the table
when I saw fluttering in the jar.

'It's your caterpillar woken up,'
said the teacher. Straightaway
I wanted to go home
to bring fresh leaves,
but she said, 'No,

you must go to your garden
where you found him
and set him free
among the raspberry leaves
to lay his eggs.'

Just for that day
we kept him in the jar
to see his coloured wings,
then I went home
and took off the lid.

Ever since that time
there have been caterpillars
on our raspberry leaves.
He made a good job
of laying those eggs.

# Where Miss Apple Goes

Nobody knows
where Miss Apple
goes at night.
    Maybe home
    to an orchard
    of apple trees
    where she sees
        green fruit
        by moonlight;
        sleeps,
        dreaming of apples
        with childrens' faces
        all in a row;
            comes to school,
            cool as a breeze,
            to see if it's so.

# In the Playground

## A Nut up my Nose

In the playground Tracey Smith
shoved a nut up my nose.
She said, 'I'll give you a surprise;
open your mouth and close your eyes!'
Then she stuffed it up my nose,
and it wouldn't come down.

I decided to tell the teacher.
'Please, there's a nut up my nose.'
'Sit down!' she said.
'You should have started writing.'
I tried poking with my pencil,
trying to get it down.

Coming home I told my sister,
'There's a nut up my nose.'
'Mum will be cross,' she said.
So I watched Dangermouse
and blew my nose into a tissue,
but it didn't come down.

At bedtime I told my mum,
'There's a nut up my nose.
A girl in the playground pushed it up.'
'Is this true?' she asked,
then fetched the vacuum cleaner,
tried to suck it down.

At the hospital Mum told the nurse,
'There's a nut up his nose.
A girl at school pushed it up.'
She shone a little torch
and tried with tweezers;
it wouldn't come down.

'Doctor, this young patient
has a nut up his nose.'
'Take him to Casualty,' he ordered,
'I'll boil up my instruments.'
I blew hard in my hanky,
but it didn't come down.

Soon he came back. 'Now for the boy
with a nut up his nose.'
He had a long needle with a tiny hook.
'Don't worry, this won't hurt.'
And there it was, in the palm of his hand,
safely come down.

Mum wrote a note: 'Yesterday
John had a nut up his nose.'
The teacher said, 'Why didn't you tell me?
Nuts are easy, if you don't poke them.
Just a gentle squeeze,
you can make them come down.'

# Trouble

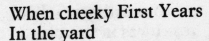

When cheeky First Years
In the yard
    Start acting hard
    They soon find out
    I'm trouble.

Choosing
A football team at school?
Make me the Captain!
That's the rule,
Or I'll make trouble.

Those sweets you've brought
To give away;
Remember,
I'm your best friend today,
Or there'll be trouble.

Nobody refuses me a thing;
I'm always the boss,
The ace, the king.
Try me.
I'm trouble.

# Sailing my Boat

Yesterday at school
I was in trouble
for sailing my yacht
in the playground.

When it rains
a deep lake appears
in the corner of the yard;
I took my boat, for some fun.

BUT, Miss Apple saw me
and said, 'Nobody
is allowed to sail boats
in the playground.'

At tea I told my dad
about the new lake.
He said, 'Let's go
and try your sailing boat.'

We had a good time,
me and my dad,
floating the yacht
across the wide water.

Today there's only mud.
Miss Apple has told everyone
they're not to play there,
even wearing boots.

I think I'll tell my dad
tonight, about the mud;
maybe he'd like to see it.
We could bring our Wellingtons.

# Nobody to Play With

Susan told Tracey
that I called Jane a fat cow,
but it was Amanda –
Julie heard her say it
to Alison –
so then Jane wouldn't play with me.

Next day Amanda let me hold
her skipping rope, with Alison,
because Tracey was away,
but Susan and Jane and Julie
wouldn't skip,
so Amanda went off with them.

I wanted to look for them
but Alison said, 'We can skip
tomorrow, when Tracey comes back.'
So we shared our sweets.
I'm going to Alison's house tonight,
to play with her.

# Flying

Every time
The wind is high,
Terry Ashworth
Tries to fly.

He fastens a pole
Across his back,
Makes wings with a pair
Of polythene sacks,

And rushes
Up and down the yard,
Trying hard
To have lift-off.

But although
We all of us
Give him space,
And he travels
At a terrific pace,

He always stays
With his feet
On the ground;
He says it's his boots
That hold him down.

# Out and About

## Weather
*Based on a traditional skipping rhyme*

All in together, girls,
Never mind the weather, girls,
Along comes the bogeyman
Who lives in the wind;

Crashing down the roof slates,
Swinging on the garden gates,
Dancing in the trousers
On the washing line.

All in together, girls,
Never mind the weather, girls,
Along comes the bogeyman
Who lives in the rain;

Chuckling in the waterspouts,
Putting all the fires out,
Drumming with his fingers
On the windowpane.

All in together, girls,
Never mind the weather, girls,
Along comes the bogeyman
Who lives in the snow;

Sitting on the privet hedge,
Covering the flower beds,
All the hungry little birds
Go 'cheep, cheep, cheep!'

All in together, girls,
Never mind the weather, girls,
Never mind the bogeyman,
He's fast asleep.

# Butterfly Calypso

Plenty butterflies
warm their wings
on this bank, man.
Plenty butterflies
warm their wings
on this bank.

Lightly landin',
the brambles
give them no grief, man.
They tiptoe tread
like a lady dance
on a leaf.

Paper ladies,
they powder, paint
on this bank, man.
Sun is shinin',
they warm their wings
on this bank.

# Easy Mover

I'm a switchback ride
On a sky-high track;
I'm a nippy little racer
With the roof turned back.

I'm the London-Glasgow
Midnight flyer,
Rushing down the rails
Like a forest fire.

If you see me coming
Take to your heels;
I'm the one and only
Poem on wheels!

# Storm

'CRASH!' says the thunder.
'I'm boss of you all.
Move over, mountains,
You're standing too tall!'

He bullies the clouds
Until they weep.
'Sssshhh!' say the trees,
'We're trying to sleep.'

# Ginger

>Mrs Garter who lives
>at twenty-nine
>has a ginger cat
>who is very fine.

In fact, he is absolutely enormous!

>I heard Mrs Garter
>tell my mum
>that he weighs two stones;
>I can believe it.

That cat must be a record-breaker!

>Each evening
>when we're playing out,
>Mrs Garter shouts
>to him, 'Ginger!'

He knows his name, but he doesn't go running.

>Standing there
>with her little dish,
>she calls, 'Ginger,
>come for your lovely fish!'

He sits round the corner, pretending not to hear.

    He can afford to wait
because he's already
had one tea
with us,

    and one at Ashworth's
and at Kenworthy's,
and Binns',
and a few scraps at Bakers' . . .

# Brave

Geronimo, swinging by rope
across the stream
from tree to tree,

loses one shoe in the mud,
kicks the other one
after it,

flings himself astride
his bucking bronco bicycle.
Geronimo!

# Countdown

'Dial,' said the poster,
'6 5 4 3 2 1
for an unforgettable
experience.'

I lifted the receiver,
put money
in the slot, dialled
the number.

The phone box
TOOK OFF!

Thundering flames
shot me upwards
into the circle
of a sapphire sky;

above trees, houses,
traffic, people,
beyond birds,
beyond clouds;

into the clear
blue stratosphere
without a ticket –
I'm still up here,

leaving Earth
at the speed of light,
sending this message
by satellite.